Find yourself being lost

Taylor Sharp

Presentation by *BookLeaf Publishing*

Web: www.bookleafpub.com

E-mail: info@bookleafpub.com

ISBN: 9789357696760

First edition 2022

DEDICATION

I'd like to take the opportunity to loosely dedicate this book to the following;

Those who raised me strong, Those who raised me wrong,

Those that weren't there for me and the ones who still are, all of the above should know who you are...

You've broke me but saved me because without the life I've lived, I'd never have known this strength and find the power to live.

A seed

Soaking up the warmth of life, Growing under all
conditions, Soils rich, not ill, just listen,
Ignore the truth, keep growing... Transition.
Now your bigger, stronger too- but along with that
must come the truth..
The soils tainted and so are you, that's why you've
grown, into what's come to.
But all will be revived, you know that it's true,
After heavy rain, some sun must come too.. So don't
fall down and become wilted up,
Your a seed once sowed,
In time things go up.

Tired

You spend so long running,
From the evil that's so succumbing,
Always looking left to right,
Actions leading to oversight,
You spend your days trying hard,
Feed what's left to others with no regard, Solving
problems, but never your own,
I don't remember a time a place felt like home
All this running to find my place had left me lost
beyond all faith..
So I must stop running,
and let myself rest.
Enjoy the walk,
for more and for less,
Because at the end of the day running away has
brought me no joy, no closure..
Just dismay.

Sometimes..

Sometimes I wonder why I was chosen,
To be one of many who are lost and unspoken..
What did I do to deserve this pain?
Something I've never had explained..
Why did they do it, how could he be so cruel?
Sometimes those who are closest, teach more then
you learn in school..
So wearily now I tread, for who can be trusted?
..Mistreated, left tread on, abused, mistrusted,
Lied to, led on, beaten and busted..
Sometimes I wonder if I'll ever discover, the peace of
no over analysation,
the apprehension,
fear of another..

Waves

Confused and sad, lost and angry,
Emotions often crash down like crazy.
One day all there, sometimes just few,
Humongous waves, seemingly impossible to break
through..
Sometimes I'm drowning, sometimes ashore,
Sometimes I'm just wading, waiting, unsure..
But at the end of the day we all learn to swim..

Just like the waves keep rolling and the tide comes in,
things eventually settle,
don't let the ocean win.

Trapped

Stuck in a corner, nowhere to turn,
Looking for family, a safe place I yearn.
But that doesn't come free, we're not all that blessed, all
you can do is show them your best..
Hold your head high for it's not all your fault,
They forget the abuse, the starvation, the assault.. they'll
push you down and make you feel trapped, that's what they
are best at, narcissistic attacks..
They leave you trapped, thinking your broken, stuck in a
pattern of internalised emotions..
But trust me when I say it's them and not you,
As a human your a product of what your subjected to..
They can trap you and belittle, but your not under their
spell, be strong, break those bonds and traps that bind you
to hell.

Thoughts

I sit at night all alone,
That's when my thoughts go to my old home..
Life so dark, everything so bleak,
My optimism for my future growing weak..
Why did it happen? Why me?
Why did it destroy what I call family..
My thoughts led to be destructive,
leaving me broken and unproductive,
so I try and try harder to find answers the mixed
questions..

But that's the thing about thoughts..
they shape your perception.
You can't let them wander, remind yourself how far
you've come and how far you'll go in yonder,
Change directions.

Alone

Small, surrounded by siblings and parents,
all that lost, sent to a new residence..
Who are these people? Where is my family?
Does anybody care? Why did they abandon me?
 Your too much too handle, so go you must, once again
losing all trust..
Hello new caregivers, will you love me? Am I safe? Are
my parents still thinking of me?
... No you can't see them, and no we don't love you, we just
get paid to take care of you..
Troubled you are, too much stress, so now your sent to a
new address..
Hello new carers, I'm sorry I don't trust, I'll try be to be
quiet, be good, I must...
"You don't have to be sorry, it's okay to be hurt, your safe
and your loved and we'll help you and make this work"
For once I felt safety, loved and secure...
Only for that to become obscured...
Not by choice, but by force of the devil, who couldn't live
with his actions and projected his predatory level..
Off I go again heartbroken and lost, this is when I lost all
trust.
All alone, thirteen by now, nobody to teach me, to love me
and show me how, so alone I stayed still surrounded by ill
people teaching myself to never surrender to their evil.

Promises

Promises are magical,
full of hope and wonder,
excitement,
a bonding moment with a special one another
....

But promises get broken and those people still love,
little do you know hurt deep down,
Just saying "no probs"
But one broken promise can lead to two, one more
here, another one there,
All of a sudden lost faith in you...
Loving you still but knowing you won't be there,
craving your support your love and your care.

Our Environment

Two people put in the same bad environment,
They watched how they changed,
One withdrawn, one violent..
Day by day these conditions shaping you, changing
your personality, your views, who you both turn into..
Two ends of the spectrum clashing together, lost in
life but bonded together,
Sometimes you'll agree and sometimes you won't,
but no matter what,
We can't give up, we won't. xx

Love and loss

Love is crazy, takes over your soul, makes you forgive,
see things that aren't whole,
And then you experience loss,
And that's a whole different thing,
It can make you hate yourself, the world,
entirely everything..
Both feelings so strong,
In each their own way,
Sometimes these two will lead you astray..

Love,
You have all hope,
everything's great,
until it turns bad.. your worried about your fate.

Loss,
You lose all hope,
Everything's lost,
Your heart physically ripped open no way to move past.

..But no matter how different each one makes you feel,
At the end of the day your truth will reveal,
You'll remember your love for the loss and the loss in your
love,
Each night you think.. As you stare above,
Slowly learning, Time passing,
You'll realise life's happenings,
There's good and there's bad in every situation,
it's just how you judge that and your own navigation.

Losing a parent

Losing a parent comes in many forms,
But me myself, the things that hit raw,
Is the fact your alive, you were supposed to protect
me, instead you intruded, assaulted and neglected
me..
Kept me stuck in your mental grip,
Losing all contact with friends and family.. mental
slip
....
Months and months of hiding in bed, listening to
your dark thoughts coming out of your mouth,
instead of staying in your head.
Subjected to views no teenager should see, scaring
me, trapping me, scarring me..
I barricaded my door and hid in the shower knowing
you were always watching in control I had lost any
power..
You handed me a bullet with my name written on it,
left me to get so sick and hospitalised I was scared I
might have offed it.
...

 I got out of there and never got justice, Living my
life broken, feeling disgusted..
But you made me feel that way, I never asked for
this, you crossed a line and left me dismissed..

One day you'll face the wrath of your inhumane
decisions, exposed to the world how you treated me
and conditioned.
Until that day comes,
I hope you never sleep at night and if you ever dream
of your lost daughter,
 it gives you a fright.

Chemical balance

"Your depressed?
Let me assist you,
Take this little pill it'll help fix you.."
"This one doesn't work, I don't feel okay, I don't want
to take medicine just to be free in a way"
"But no you must take it, they take a while to work"
"But holding on hurts and nothing you've been giving
me has worked"
"Things will get better you just have to have hope"
..while they hand me the pills that make me want to
use a rope...
"They're still not working, will nobody listen?" "Your
unreceptive, recovery is a lot of your decision"
I can't stop my brain feeling this way, please won't
you just, ...take my life away?

Dazed

Ever since I was young,
I remember the feeling of being numb..
Walking around in a daze, just complying, lost in
pain,
Along with hatred and regret too..
How come I can't connect with you, or you or you?
See you either go with or against the flow,
I went with it, but little did they know ..
That underneath I seen it all,
I wasn't too young I remember it all..
So many reasons to want to leave but stuck here
dazed , uncared for till he became deceased..
Then it all changed I never seen you,
but still not raised properly....
dazed still,
confused.

Pillow Stains

For so long they fell,
Throat closing and choking,
Eyes turning into a well,
Salty sadness falling with other emotions too,
Nobody to care for me, I don't know how to fix it
who can I turn to...?
... The soft fluffy whiteness when you rest down your
head cuddle me tight and release what's in your head..
Drown me in tears and let it all go, nobody hears you,
tomorrow it won't show..
Nobody will see what's underneath my slip, Like you
my dear there's stains left missed,
But just like me it won't last forever those stains shall
be replaced with something much better.

Window view

As I look out the window,
upon the other kids playing,
I wonder what their view is like from where I am laying,
Do they have lots of friends?
A comfortable bed?
A warm meal at night,
somebody to kiss their head?
Things still change but the view not so much,
Just a different window frame now,
Further out of touch,
Growing but not learning any of the right things, lost in the
system, trying to spread my wings..
But in the room always stuck looking out the window the
view never changing much..

Then I got older, released from that cocoon, Wings spread
wide... left me back in that room.
Had to lay and watch and be ready again to spread my
wings and learn times ten,
Now I've seen more then I care for but atleast I can say I'm
no longer stuck staring out the windowsills bay.

Clay

Squeeze it in your hand,
Manipulate its shape,
Turn it into something different,
Be amazed at its fate..
Just like humans I guess the same can be said,

 Be careful how you hold things,

You could be making it, or breaking it instead.

Ripple

Throw a massive rock into the waters,
Watch all the ripples and sudden disorder,
Underneath the surface tadpoles trying to grow,
one hit from the rock,
others still trying throughout trauma though..

Two little tadpoles learnt hard and fast how to
swim, but maturing under hard conditions still
creates thick skin..
Eventually matured into fully grown frogs,
stronger then the others with the highest hops.

Unpacking

I opened the door to my younger self,
Unpacking all that's on the shelf,
I cried and laughed and retreated again,
Learning all of what I'd held onto times ten,
As much as it hurt,
I inspected it all,
re learning,
re living,
Until i could face it for new beginnings.